# The Wheel of Life

Kulananda

# The Wheel of Life

WINDHORSE PUBLICATIONS

*Also by Kulananda*
Principles of Buddhism
Teachers of Enlightenment
Western Buddhism

Published by Windhorse Publications, 11 Park Road, Birmingham, B13 8AB
www.windhorsepublications.com

© Kulananda 2000

Printed by Interprint Ltd, Marsa, Malta
Cover design: Karmabandhu
Cover images: from a thangka painted by Jampa Tseundu, courtesy of Akasasuri and Varamitra, photograph by Moksajyoti, © Clear Vision Trust Picture Archive

*A catalogue record for this book is available from the British Library.*
ISBN 1 899579 30 3

The right of Kulananda to be identified as the author of this work has been asserted by him in accordance with the Copyright, Designs and Patents Act 1988

Since this work is intended for a general readership, Pali and Sanskrit words have been transliterated without the diacritical marks which would have been appropriate in a work of a more scholarly nature.

The publishers acknowledge with gratitude permission to quote from the following:
p.43: from Buddhaghosa, *The Path of Purification*, trans. Bhikkhu Nanamoli, Buddhist Publication Society, Kandy 1991.
p.59: We quote by permission of the Pali Text Society which owns the copyright in Buddhaghosa, *The Atthasalini*, trans. Maung Tin, in *The Expositor*, ed. C.A.W. Rhys Davids, Pali Text Society, London 1920.
p.62: We quote by permission of the Pali Text Society which owns copyright in F.L. Woodward (trans.), *The Book of Gradual Sayings, Anguttara Nikaya*, Pali Text Society, Oxford 1996.

# CONTENTS

*About the Author*

Kulananda was born Michael Chaskalson, in South Africa in 1954. He migrated to England in 1972, where he encountered the Friends of the Western Buddhist Order (FWBO) while studying for a philosophy degree at the University of East Anglia in 1976. Ordained in 1977, he has since devoted himself to the development of the Western Buddhist Order and the FWBO. He has played a key part in the development of several FWBO Right Livelihood enterprises (including Windhorse Trading, now perhaps the largest Buddhist Right Livelihood business in the West), as well as several Buddhist centres. He was, for a time, secretary to Sangharakshita, the founder of the Order, and is now a member of the FWBO's Preceptors' College Council, the body to whom Sangharakshita has handed over his official responsibilities. At present he spends most of his time writing, teaching, and maintaining his contacts with the those FWBO centres of which he is president.

He has written three previous books: *Western Buddhism* and *Principles of Buddhism* are published by Thorsons, and *Teachers of Enlightenment* is published by Windhorse Publications.

# PREFACE

IN THE MID-EIGHTIES I visited the Basilica di San Marco in Venice with my friend Devamitra. In the square next to the basilica itself stands the great tower of the campanile. Its construction began in the year 912, and it stood for nearly ten centuries until, in 1902, it outdid Pisa's Leaning Tower by actually toppling over into the square. The city council met to decide what to do, and sagely agreed to rebuild it *com'era, dov'era* – as it was, where it was – with the addition of an internal lift.

My friend and I passed into the basilica itself, with its floor of inlaid marble and glass glowing in the restricted light of the great church. The walls are decorated throughout with mosaics, and with many varieties of marble. These mosaics, all of them on a golden ground, represent numerous scenes and incidents from the Christian tradition. As I walked from one to the next, I became aware that the whole interior was a kind of giant storybook, through which believers had learned and contemplated the heritage of their faith over many centuries.

Buddhism, too, communicates its truths in pictures as well as in words. One also finds temples in many parts of the East richly decorated with murals. Some depict incidents from the life of the Buddha or another great Dharma practitioner. Others represent the brilliant figures of archetypal Buddhas and Bodhisattvas. This is because Buddhist teachers have always understood the necessity of speaking the language of symbols as well as that of words. We human beings are multifaceted, and the world of reason is but one of the realms we inhabit. As Buddhism aims at total self-transformation, it has to address men and women in all their various aspects. The language of symbols is crucial to this task.

In this small book, the second in the series on Buddhist symbols, Kulananda explores one of the most important visual depictions of the Buddhist understanding of life. It is not pure symbol, for some of its elements are more like pictorial reminders of the Dharma than true symbols. Nevertheless, its parts add up to one of the most complex and subtle representations of the nature of the mind that can be found in any spiritual tradition. And it does have strong symbolic value. The wheel is itself a powerful symbol. While it can be a positive image, in the case of the Wheel of Life the stress falls on its qualities of limitation and repetition. The Wheel of Life shows us how we repeat (or even how we *are*) limiting patterns based on a constricted understanding of life and of our own minds.

If we look honestly at our lives, we see all too often that we repeat the same ingrained habits. This compulsion causes us suffering. From time to time the castles in the air we have envisaged – or the ivory towers into which we have tried to retreat – come crashing down. But rather than seeing their limitations, we feel compelled to rebuild them. Usually, because we do not understand the nature of the forces that drive us, we end up repeating the same mistakes. We find ourselves rebuilding our life as it was, where it was.

Contemplating the Wheel of Life, with Kulananda's skilful guidance, we can learn to recognize the hindering forces at work in our minds, and begin to liberate ourselves. Not for nothing is this Wheel traditionally displayed at the entrance to a temple. It symbolically shows us what it is we need to leave behind in order to draw near to sacred space. The Wheel is an image of unsatisfactoriness, even suffering. Dwelling upon it can motivate us to approach the temple of the depths of consciousness. More than that, its contemplation can give us the understanding that enables us to gain entry to that temple, for the Wheel of Life is not simply an elegant analysis of why we find life unsatisfactory: as you will see, it contains within it the keys to its own transcendence.
*Vessantara, Birmingham, August 2000*

# 1

## INTRODUCTION

WHY AM I LIKE THIS? There are six billion human beings on this planet and countless other forms of sentient life. How come I have turned out to be just this one, who thinks, feels, speaks, and sees things in one unique way, different from every other living being? The symbol we know in the West as the Wheel of Life, known in Sanskrit as the *bhavachakra*, or Wheel of Becoming, sets out to answer this question, and in the process it tells us much else besides.

I remember the first time I came upon a depiction of the Wheel, taped to the crumbling white wall of a squat in London, its edges torn and curling. We would lie under it and, under the influence of one or another psychotropic substance, dream our dreams of freedom. At that time, I didn't understand its significance. A monster held fast to a large disk that was divided into several segments in which weird, mysterious, things happened – people were chopped into bits, women gave birth, animals romped and frolicked, armies fought, demons tortured people, a couple made love.... It never occurred to me to find out what it all meant. Those sort of questions were not really cool. It was a mandala, so much I knew, and mandalas were associated with Tibetan Buddhism, as in *The Tibetan Book of the Dead*, as in Timothy Leary's psychedelic maps of consciousness, as on the cover of Ram Das's *Be Here Now*. That was enough. The main thing was, and no one could deny this, it was really exotic.

If only I had known then what I know now – that the Wheel was not really a poster, torn and grubby, Sellotaped on to a pockmarked wall – but rather it was a mirror, reflecting back at us all the many states that we passed through, as we lay on Indian bedspreads under its steady gaze. Mute, unable to speak its wisdom until we found out more, that frail, curling image of the Wheel might have told us that all things that arise will pass away; that our minds determine the way we are now, the way we have been, and the way we will become. It would also have told us that we can change ourselves for the better. We cycle in a great round of re-becoming – the Wheel would have told us – over and over again, passing through world after world, mental state after mental state, life after life. Endlessly revolving in states of dissatisfaction, this process rolls on and on, indefinitely, until we take hold, wake up, and start to take our destiny in our own hands.

The Wheel reveals how this all works. It shows us who we now are; how things came to be as they are for us; and how we can change them for the better. Stuck on that crumbling wall, the Wheel was a mirror waiting to be looked into; a map waiting to be followed.

The origins of the Wheel of Life, as a developed symbol, lie far back in Buddhist history. Ancient Indian canonical texts[1] contain instructions for its graphic representation, and one example, dating from the sixth century, has been preserved on a wall in one of the Buddhist caves at Ajanta, in India. These days, its use continues to be very widespread in Tibetan Buddhism, and now it has come to the West.

One of the chief functions of the Wheel is to describe the processes whereby we cycle in 'the round of rebirth'. All the great Buddhist teachers, from the Buddha onwards, have taught that unenlightened sentient beings are caught up in a vast process of constant rebirth. We die and are reborn, over and over and over....

This is not to say that we ourselves, as we now are, are reborn with just the same habits and characteristics we exhibit in the present. Nor is it to suggest that we have, somewhere, somehow, a fixed, essential essence – something like a 'soul' – that is immortal and always reincarnates after the death of the body. The Buddhist view is more subtle than that. There is change and there is continuity. In dependence upon what went before, arises what comes next. This is a universal truth taught by the Buddhas. But what comes next is not exactly the same, in any respect, as what went before. Everything changes – all the time. So, in dependence upon what I am at the moment of my death, what I will be at the first flickering moment of consciousness in my next rebirth arises. It is like a flame passing through a bundle of twigs. The flame is never the same flame. Passing from twig to twig, it changes constantly. But there is continuity: although it changes, there is still a flame.

From lifetime to lifetime we are born and reborn, over and over. The Wheel of Life just keeps revolving. We can understand this teaching in two ways. Macrocosmically, we can take it as saying that we move from physical birth to physical death to physical rebirth, over and over again. Or, microcosmically, we can understand it as saying that we continually move from one mental state to another, in a process of constant change in the course of a single lifetime – even in the course of a few moments.

But whether we see it macrocosmically or microcosmically, one thing is certain. Like everything else, we are constantly changing. The Wheel of Life describes the mechanisms that govern the deepest levels of this process of change. Basic Buddhist thought discerns two profoundly different ways of being. The very large majority of us experience the world in terms of a constant reaction between two polar opposites. We experience some pleasure, but in time it gives way to pain. Happiness gives way to sorrow, sorrow to happiness. Not knowing the true nature of reality, we cycle seemingly endlessly between the poles of joy and sadness. This cyclic tendency is the process of *Samsara*, which is life as most of us know it, a continual revolving, from which the image of the Wheel derives. Birth gives way to death, death to birth, round and around, over and over. But besides this 'samsaric' process there is also a 'nirvanic' process.

Nirvana, 'blowing out', is a synonym for Enlightenment. It represents the extinction of all the drives towards self-centredness that foster unenlightened delusion and keep us trapped on the Wheel. Free from delusion, motivated by friendliness, generosity, and wisdom, the Enlightened person acts in the world solely for the benefit of others. The path of the spiritual life, the 'nirvanic' process, leads onwards and upwards, away from the Wheel, towards Enlightenment.

The Wheel of Life shows us how the cyclic processes of Samsara work, and it points out the path to Nirvana.

Underlying the whole conception of the Wheel of Life is the Buddhist idea of karma. This idea is often understood as a principle of retributive justice that determines a person's state of life. This is not the Buddhist view. In Buddhism, karma means more like 'willed action', and the Buddhist theory of karma tells us simply that all willed acts, of body, speech, or mind, inevitably have outcomes, and that the quality of those outcomes, whether they contain joy or grief, will depend upon the mental state that motivated them. Positive mental states such as kindness, clarity, and generosity, give rise to acts that have beneficial consequences. Negative mental states, such as animosity, confusion, and meanness lead to acts that have harmful outcomes. The Wheel of Life shows some of the ways in which the mechanism of karma operates.

There is no single agreed version of the Wheel of Life, but the one described in this book contains all the elements that are most commonly found. Before going on to examine the components of this great symbol in more detail, I will first of all very briefly introduce the chief elements of the Wheel as found in our illustration.

The Wheel itself is divided into four concentric circles. At the hub, we find a cock, a snake, and a pig, each biting the tail of the one in front. These three animals represent, respectively, craving, aversion, and spiritual ignorance.

The next segment is divided in two, one half black, one white. In the white segment, beings – in accordance with their skilful deeds – ascend to heavenly worlds. In the black segment, because of their unskilful acts, they plunge downward into the hells.

The next circle, which is by far the largest, is divided into six segments. These depict the six primary modes of being – or realms – within which consciousness can manifest. These are, starting from the top and proceeding clockwise, the realms of the gods, the titans, the hungry ghosts, the hell beings, the animals, and the humans.

In our illustration a Buddha appears in each of these realms. This is the Bodhisattva Avalokiteshvara, the embodiment of the compassionate aspect of Enlightenment. In each realm he holds up an object that shows what the beings there need in order to take the next step in their spiritual development.

The final circle of the Wheel, its rim, is divided into twelve segments. These depict various stages in the process of *pratitya-samutpada*, or 'conditioned co-production'. This describes the process by which we and the realms we inhabit arise and pass away in dependence on ever-changing conditions.

In the first segment, a blind man with a stick gropes his way forward. This describes the state of spiritual ignorance in which all unenlightened beings find themselves. Next, a potter throws pots on a wheel. This describes our *samskaras*, our 'karma formations', the deep habitual processes that underlie our actions. Then we see a monkey climbing a flowering tree; a boat with four passengers, one of whom is steering; and a house with five windows and a door. These represent consciousness; the five *skandhas* – the basic constituents of the psychophysical organism; and the six sense organs (in Buddhism, mind is a sixth sense organ). Then we see a man and woman embracing, followed by a man with an arrow in his eye, symbolizing sense contact and feeling. Next, a woman offers a drink to a seated man – thirst or craving; a man gathers fruit from a tree – grasping; and a pregnant woman represents 'becoming'. In the last two segments we see a woman giving birth and a corpse – representing birth and death.

The whole Wheel is grasped tightly in the hands and jaws of a great monster – Yama, the Lord of Death – who stands for the great inescapable fact of universal impermanence. In a sense, Yama has two faces. Holding up the Wheel, we see him in his traditional, wrathful, form. Here he is witness to the fact that all things whatever are subject to change and to becoming other. We crave security, yearn for the known, and never wish to lose the pleasant things or experiences that we have. As a result, we suffer. But Yama also stands for the possibility of change for the better. Because things are impermanent, because they always change, every situation can be improved and we ourselves can grow and change for the better.

What exactly such change for the better might mean is hinted at in the final two symbols. In the top right-hand corner we see a Buddha figure, and in the top left-hand corner a white full moon, containing the figure of a hare. In the West we have a man-in-the-moon; in parts of the East they have a hare. The story of how this came about is as follows.

Once there was a hare, who sacrificed himself to feed a hungry guest.[2] The guest, in this case, turned out to be the great god Indra, in disguise, and the hare was the Buddha-to-be, who was still pursuing his Bodhisattva career. Indra restored the hare to life and drew his picture in the full moon, where it can be seen even today – a constant reminder of the Bodhisattva's spirit of generosity and self-sacrifice.

The Buddha, pointing out the hare in the moon, indicates the Bodhisattva path. The cultivation of a deeply altruistic attitude, he tells us, is the way to escape from the Wheel. How we go about doing that, however, depends to some extent on our understanding of how things are and how they come to be.

For this reason, the Wheel of Life is a symbol of tremendous spiritual significance. We can use it to help locate ourselves – to see ourselves, to some extent at least – as we really are. We will then know not only what we have to do, but also how to go about doing it.

# 2

## THE HUB

THE COCK, THE SNAKE, AND THE PIG – craving, aversion, and delusion – who chase one another round and around the hub of the Wheel, represent the fundamental driving forces of Samsara. The red cock, a symbol of both greed and lust, constantly scratches about in the earth looking for food, the green snake glares with venomous, hate-filled eyes, and the black pig wallows in the mud of ignorance. Each bites tightly the tail of the one in front – greedy, hateful, and blind.

These 'three poisons' – craving, aversion, and delusion – are inextricably interlinked. When we act from greed we hate what stands in our way and reinforce our fundamental ignorance. This is ignorance of the fact that the mundane world can never completely fulfil our desires, that all our suffering is caused by our craving, that happiness comes from the ending of craving, and that there is a path we can follow that leads to the cessation of craving.

Ignorant of these facts, unable or unwilling to bear them in mind, we constantly act, speak, and think in ways that simply do not help us. Dissatisfied with my current state of boredom, I switch on the television and mindlessly take in a few moments of soap opera before wandering down to the kitchen to put on a bit of surplus weight for the sake of a fleeting sense experience (toast and honey). Then I drift back to the sitting room to make a phone call to a friend where I speak sarcastically of a mutual acquaintance who irritates me. And so it goes on. Over and over, round and around. Craving, aversion, craving, aversion. Fleeting mental state after mental state. Acting like this I keep myself mildly anaesthetized, taking in this, pushing out that, driven from moment to moment by an underlying sense of dissatisfaction that I am unwilling fully to face up to.

The Buddha never condemned craving, aversion, and delusion as sinful. They are simply a part of the way things are, a part of the way *we* are, but, he said, if we wish to escape from suffering we must free ourselves from their bonds. This is not easy, for the three poisons lie at the very root of Samsara.

For any organism to exist at all, two essential factors must be present. The organism must have a boundary around it, so that we can say 'this, the organism, is what is inside the boundary, the rest of the world is outside of it.' Then it must have the capacity to keep this boundary more or less intact by taking into itself what it needs for its survival and by pushing away from itself anything that threatens it. This is true of all organisms whatsoever: human beings, giraffes, goldfish, and single-celled amoebas, as well as cities, countries, and public corporations. Animals that cannot feed or defend themselves become food for other animals. Countries that cannot do so are absorbed by their stronger neighbours. Taking in what is needed and pushing out that which threatens are intrinsically necessary to all forms of existence.

But what of the boundary? This, in a sense, is the essence of the unenlightened human problem. For although, in order to survive in an ordinary way, we need to take in nourishment and push out what threatens, we end up taking our own boundaries far too seriously. We treat them as if they were fixed and unchanging, and so we live our lives confined entirely within the boundary of our skin, as if we were somehow essentially separate from all the rest of life. And thus the three poisons have us in their thrall.

Experiencing ourselves as fixed and separate, cut off in some deep sense from other people and from the rest of our environment, consciously or not, we feel threatened and insecure. We are just one tiny, insignificant, changing being adrift in a vast universe of potentially threatening otherness. We are small and relatively powerless, what is not us is immense and hugely powerful. Seeing ourselves in this way, our natural tendency is to overemphasize the process of taking in and pushing out. We try to take into ourselves as much as we can of whatever we think will give us security – food, comfort, and status – and to push away from ourselves whatever appears to threaten these. We do all of this under the delusion that we *are* ultimately fixed and separate, that getting more of Samsara is better, and that we can preserve our imagined separateness from the rest of life by constantly keeping threats at bay.

This process is intrinsically unstable, for we are not fixed and unchanging entities. Like everything else in the universe we are constantly changing, even from instant to instant. Our vain attempts to resist change by leading our lives in safe, familiar ruts, or by pursuing neurotic habits like comfort eating and leisure shopping, dam up our energies and generate suffering for ourselves and others. Even if we own the latest style trainers and always drink great cappuccino, as long as we depend on these experiences for our sense of inner worth and psychological security, our position will remain fundamentally untenable. Even those who live their lives at the very pinnacle of fashion will one day sicken and die.

The secure sense of ourselves as somehow fixed and complete – separate from the rest of life – that we constantly try to achieve, is impossible to attain in the face of reality. For ultimately we can never be separate. From moment to moment we affect and are affected by everything else in our environment. The air we breathe, the food we eat, the impressions and ideas that we take in, all come from outside ourselves. There is nothing within us that is not affected by the continual process of exchange between ourselves and our environment.

The world we move in is a constantly swirling mass of change. But having constructed for ourselves a fixed sense of the world where we, as more or less bounded and unchanging subjects, interact with a stable world of objects, we experience a constant friction between things as they are and the world of our delusions. Bumping up against reality but unwilling to face up to it, we suffer time after time. Only by letting go of our delusive clinging will we ever be free from suffering.

Craving, aversion, and delusion have deep roots within our psyche. The cock, the snake, and the pig drive the very hub of the Wheel. Between them they condition much of the way in which we see the world and much of our behaviour. They are the source of all our suffering, but, the Buddha assured us, they can be transformed. Greed can change into generosity, hatred can change into compassion, and ignorance can change into wisdom.

To make such changes takes consistent effort over time, perhaps even over lifetimes, but it can be done. Not only that; it can also be done by degrees. As soon as we start to make a serious effort to undermine the roots of the three poisons within us by practising the Buddhist path of ethics, meditation, and wisdom, we will immediately begin to progress. Craving, aversion, and delusion are not our only motivations; we also have within us a desire for the good, and when we give rein to that desire then the driving force at the hub of the Wheel begins to slow down. Less driven by blind craving and aversion we become increasingly conscious of the prospect of true liberation, and our hearts come to yearn more for this than for the familiarity of craving.

Cultivating generosity, kindness, and clarity, we can begin to tread the path of the Buddhist spiritual life, the altruistic path that the Buddha indicates when he points, as he does in our illustration, to the hare in the moon. Our progression along that path may be swift, or it may be slow, but one thing we can be sure of – so long as we make an effort, progress itself is assured.

# 3

## THE BLACK AND WHITE SEGMENTS

THE SYMBOLISM in this part of the Wheel is about as stark as it can get. It is laid out, literally, in black and white – light and dark. Buddhism does not speak of acts being good or bad, instead they are either skilful or unskilful. Skilful acts lead to beneficial outcomes. So, in our image, beings engaging in skilful acts ascend from the depths to the heights, from the hells to the heavens. Unskilful acts lead to suffering – beings who repeatedly act in that kind of way plunge downwards into the hells.

Although our actions are rarely quite so black-and-white, and it is not always possible to make such clear-cut distinctions, it is necessary to spell out the principle of karma, as this image does, very clearly, for this is one of the defining principles underpinning all the symbolism within the Wheel of Life.

All willed acts bear fruit in time. As we will, so we become. Those acts which proceed from generosity, kindness, and clarity yield pleasant fruits; those rooted in craving, aversion, and delusion yield unwholesome ones. This is the law of karma.

*Beings are owners of their karma, heirs of their karma, karma is the womb from which they are born. Their karma is their friend and their refuge. Whatever karma they perform, good or bad, of that they will be the heirs.*[3]

Karma literally means willed action, whether of body, speech, or mind, and our acts can be broadly divided into two kinds, skilful and unskilful: those which lead towards the light of clarity and those which tend towards the darkness of confusion.

Unlike the theistic religions that underpin the traditional ethical systems of the West, Buddhism has never spoken in terms of 'good' and 'bad'. No action, in Buddhist thought, is either good or bad in and of itself. Buddhism focuses instead on the intention behind the action. What matters is the quality of our motives. This is not to say that those things we do unintentionally have no consequences. If I slip in the kitchen and spill scalding hot tea on a friend, that will certainly have consequences, but those consequences are of a completely different order to what they would be had I emptied the teapot over him deliberately. Unintentional acts do not modify our character.

We all know what it is like to have feelings of warmth and good will towards others. On a sunny day, perhaps, out for a walk in beautiful countryside with a good friend, the world is alive, sparkling with colour and birdsong, and we feel expansive and generous, fully part of the vast process of life – sensitive, adventurous, and open to new experience. We want the best for everyone, for every living thing, and acting, speaking, and thinking in that way we reinforce the good in the world we inhabit and feel less cut off from other people, less cut off from the rest of life. But we also know what it is like not to feel like that; to feel irritable and cut off from others. We feel tightly enclosed inside our skin in a world that is uncomfortable and hostile, dark and confused. Acting from feelings like these, we send our barbs out into the world and so help to keep our environment apparently hostile.

All things whatsoever are mutually interdependent. We know this almost intuitively. We see the way that leaves fall and turn into humus that enriches the soil that feeds the tree that grows the leaves that fall. We see the way we depend for our food on the farmer, the truck driver, the wholesaler, the greengrocer (and uncountable other be-ings). We know that a smile, given in passing, ripples onwards and outwards, raising the mood of the next and the next and the next person.

Thoughts like these help us foster feelings of empathy. We are not the only beings that matter. There are billions of others living on this planet and we all depend on one another in countless ways. Not only that. We all of us – all human beings at least – have the capacity to understand one another, to communicate with one another, and to feel for one another at ever deeper levels. Concerned for the well-being of others, we act skilfully, enjoy happiness, and move closer to Enlightenment.

On the other hand, the belief that we are all intrinsically separate from one another reinforces our natural tendency towards selfishness. When we see others as competing with us for scarce resources, be they food, status, power, or affection, that gives rise to intentions that are based primarily in self-concern, and unskilful acts follow. As a result we suffer and remain trapped within cyclic existence; cold, lonely, and alienated.

Buddhist ethics, therefore, starts with enlightened (small e) self-interest. If you cultivate positive intentions you will act more and more skilfully. As a result, you will move closer towards Enlightenment and you will grow happier. Living more and more in the light of clarity, leaving behind the darkness of confusion, you progressively shed the habits of deluding selfishness that cause you to suffer.

The law of karma, however, does not determine everything that happens in our world. The Buddha taught that everything arises in dependence upon preceding conditions. But the operation of conditionality is not random. It unfolds in an ordered fashion and, according to one commentarial tradition[4] there are five possible orders of conditionality. It is useful to have some rudimentary understanding of these because they help us to understand the place of karma in the natural scheme of things.

Very briefly, in ascending order of complexity, these are the physical inorganic order of conditionality that governs inanimate matter, which corresponds, more or less, to the laws of physics. Then the physical organic order governs animate matter – more or less at the level of the laws of biology. The mental order governs non-volitional mental acts, such as our feelings of hunger in the presence of food, and corresponds to certain aspects of psychology. The karmic or ethical order governs the way in which intentional acts have positive or negative consequences. And finally there is a transcendental order, which governs the later stages of the 'spiral path' that leads upwards off the Wheel, and about which we will say more later.

The law of karma, then, is part of a natural system. There is no one who apportions rewards and punishments. The system is simply the outcome of the way things are.

There is no divine ruler in Buddhism, no cosmic judge, so there is no room for any sense of sin and no idea of divine salvation. Without these, the sense of irrational guilt that plagues so many of those brought up in the West today is also removed. We are as we are. Being human, we are neither intrinsically good nor bad. But we do have choice. At every moment we can chose to act skilfully or unskilfully. We can move towards the light of clarity or remain mired in the darkness of confusion. The choice is ours and, as the black-and-white segments show, we will live with the consequences.

# 4

## THE SIX REALMS

THE NEXT CIRCLE of the Wheel is divided into six segments, each depicting one or another of the main ways in which living beings appear. Traditionally, they are spoken of as the six realms.

We can see the six realms from a psychological perspective. Here, the realms of beauty, fierce competitiveness, neurotic desire, acute torment, lazy indifference, and human creativity, show some of the different mental states we can occupy even within the course of a few hours.

Home at last from work, John puts on a Beethoven piano sonata and begins to relax. Gradually, bar after thundering bar, his mind joins with the music and he enters realms of Olympian beauty – the realm of the gods.

But, like all things, the music eventually comes to an end. Now the beginnings of boredom set in. John idly picks up the newspaper, flips through it, and suddenly his attention is caught by an advertisement. He can buy a new computer for only £1,299 … it comes with all that amazing stuff: a digital camera, scanner, colour printer – and is it fast.… Imagine what he could do with that.… Hey, then he would really get down to writing that novel.…

Now John cannot afford £1,299 just now, not after that trip to New York with Jenny, but he wants it, he really wants it. In fact, it slowly dawns on him, his life will not really be complete, *he* will not really be complete, unless he has it. If only he can get it, then he'll truly have everything he needs and his life will be completely fulfilled, he'll want for nothing, but he *must* have it. This is the realm of the pretas, of neurotic desire.

Scheming how to raise the money to buy this new computer John devises a plan to betray the confidence of Bill, one of his colleagues at the office. After all, it is a rat race out there. They are stabbing each other in the back all the time. He knows the kind of games Bill plays.... If he can be promoted above Bill, if the management knew what Bill was *really* like, then he would get that pay rise and, no problem, that new computer. Perhaps even a new car.... John has slipped into the realm of the anti-gods.

Tired out by all his scheming, feeling slightly numb, John turns on the television, then wanders off to the fridge, takes out a beer, fixes himself a snack and comes back to the sofa where he slumps back, mindlessly working his way through a plate of tortilla chips, cream cheese, and gherkin. Mildly titillated by an actress in a bikini, he sinks into an unthinking daze. This is the realm of the animals.

The phone rings and John wakes up. He has a few moments of clarity. What is he doing watching that pap on television? What a waste of time. He could have been listening to Beethoven. He could even have got back down to the first draft of the novel that has been stuck in his drawer for months now, the one that exposed the world of office politics, the one that was going to set him free from a life of drudgery. Shaking his head, back in the human realm again, John moves to the phone.

It is Jenny, and she hardly pauses to let him catch his breath. She has had enough! Their relationship is going nowhere. New York was dreadful, as he knows! He is so selfish! All he really cares about is his music and his novel (which, she adds, he will never finish anyway). In any case, she has been seeing quite a bit of Bill and they seem to understand each other so much better.... Waves of pain and jealousy wash over John. He plunges down into the realm of the hells.

And so it goes. We cycle from mental state to mental state, from one world to another, because with each new mental state the world John inhabited changed quite dramatically. When he was listening to music the world he inhabited was benign and wholesome, full of harmony and pleasure. After his phone call from Jenny it became a harsh and pain-filled place, full of suffering and discomfort.

So we can see the six realms as standing for the objective counterparts of our current psychological state, but we can also see them as inhabited by actually existing entities. Buddhism has always accepted the objective existence of beings such as gods, sprites, spirits, and demons. From the Buddhist perspective, human consciousness is not the only mode of sentient being. It is just one among a myriad possible manifestations of consciousness, each of which arises in dependence upon certain prior conditions.

Beings whose acts are consistently meritorious, and who enjoy refined states of mind, are reborn as gods. Those whose behaviour is consistently neurotic are born again as hungry ghosts – beings who are never able to satisfy their pain-filled longings.

The world as we ordinarily know it is replete with different modes of consciousness: there are cats, dogs, cows, sheep, and sparrows, to name but a few. Given our human sensory apparatus we are able to perceive these with our physical senses. But human sensory apparatus is limited and, from a Buddhist point of view, somewhat fortuitous. It just happens to be like this. Because of the way we humans have been in the past we have eyes, ears, noses, tongues, and so on, and as a result we are able to perceive certain things in certain ways. Perhaps – who knows – if we had different senses we might be able to perceive beings whose presence was not bound up with the spheres of light, sound, taste, and so on that comprise the normal limit of human perception.

The Buddha, we are told, was able to see all kinds of beings around him. Demons tried in vain to distract him and gods flocked to him for teachings. We can take stories like these literally or we can interpret them mythically. In both cases they have much to tell us. What we ought never to do is to discount them as merely simple, unsophisticated folklore or later cultural accretions on the pristine face of Buddhism. Such an approach betrays the hubris of contemporary scientific materialism – a peculiarly narrow form of literal-mindedness.

Whether we take the six realms as representing the objectively existing worlds of conscious, embodied, human and non-human beings, or whether we prefer to think of them – more psychologically – as different modes of human consciousness, the Wheel offers us a great deal of wisdom in describing what each of the realms is like. This teaching, like all others, is a tool we each need to learn to wield in our own way and for our own purposes. By learning to recognize each of the realms in our own experience we also begin to learn which realms we ought to entertain and which we ought to avoid, and we learn something of how to go about doing that as well.

# 5

## THE GODS

THIS IS A WORLD of light and colour. Its beautiful inhabitants are endowed with the highest graces. Whatever they wish for simply appears: they have no need to work. Sweet sounds fill the air and everything sparkles with a scintillating luminosity.

The word *deva*, which is usually translated as 'god', derives from a root meaning 'to shine'. The gods are the 'shining ones', radiant beings who live lives of unblemished happiness.

There are gods on earth, people to whom everything comes effortlessly and who enjoy highly refined states of mind. Some artists seem to live like this, and we can all think of people who seem somehow to be particularly favoured in their lives. They are good-looking, though not necessarily in the conventional sense, and there is something about them that just shines out. Everyone enjoys their company and they are always good to be with. Light-hearted and carefree, people like this have an aura of brightness about them that affects everyone with whom they come into contact.

In all likelihood, we ourselves have some experience of this world. Perhaps we remember times when we consistently enjoyed clearer, brighter, and more carefree mental states, or perhaps moments when we were absorbed in the appreciation of great works of art. Touching the fringes of the penetrating, refined consciousness of their creators, perhaps we entered – for a while – into their world.

The 'human' god-realm also contains those beings who, through their own spiritual efforts, have made substantial spiritual progress. They shine from within with a happiness that comes from spiritual practice. Having, through their transcendental insight, broken the fetters of habit, of a certain vagueness that always keeps all options open, and of superficiality, such beings live lives dedicated to spiritual practice – both for themselves and for others. According to the Pali tradition, such beings will be reborn on the Wheel no more than seven times.

There are also gods who are not in any sense human. Above our human world, according to the scriptural tradition, there exist plane after plane of increasingly refined states of being, all occupied by different kinds of gods. The first six of these levels, since the beings in them are still subject to subtle forms of sense desire, belong to the Wheel of Life.

Each god is embodied within a subtle physical form that is not perceivable by the usual human senses. Beautiful and noble, they experience continuous sense pleasure and satisfaction. The higher the realm, the more refined its pleasures. Each of the god worlds is traditionally shown as a kind of royal court, presided over by the chief god of that realm. Here, the gods pass their time at ease, fully absorbed in the enjoyment of beauty.

Because these gods inhabit the world of sense desire, they are able, to some extent at least, to interact with the human world. They like to visit places of natural beauty and are attracted to people who are happy and positive. They are particularly attracted to people who are practising spiritually, especially the spiritually developed, over whom they are sometimes said to cast a beneficial influence.

All the gods, however, are impermanent. Their lives are immeasurably long, and the higher the realm the longer the life, but like all other living beings the gods will die. This happens when the karma that made them gods in the first place is exhausted. None of the gods made the world and none of them presides over it indefinitely. In the *Brahmajala Sutta* of the Pali *Digha-Nikaya* the Buddha treats with gentle irony the notion of a creator god. There is a being who *thinks* he is the creator of all, the Buddha tells us, but he is deluded. He just happened to appear in his realm, through the force of previous karma, before any other beings. And when they in turn appear there, through the force of their past karma, he believes that he made them – and so do they.

Rather than being the centre of a god-made universe, the god realm for Buddhism is that world we inhabit as a result of previous skilful acts of body, speech, and mind. Skilful acts have positive consequences. Traditionally speaking, all our skilful acts create a stock of 'merit' which in time comes to fruition as a positive consequence. Gods are gods because they have accrued a great deal of merit.

The merit we generate through skilful acts may, if we have not previously created too much countervailing demerit, give rise in this life to greater ease and pleasure, or we may experience it in future heavenly rebirths. But however and wherever we experience the fruits of our skilful actions, the enjoyment and the pleasure they bring is always accompanied by the danger of intoxication. Living a life of unalloyed sensory delight, the gods are prone to forget themselves and they also lose sight of others. The existence they now enjoy is the result of their past mindfulness and ethical striving. Unless they continue to make an effort to preserve their awareness and to generate further positive karma through skilful acts, they will gradually sink to lower and lower levels of being. Eventually, it is sometimes said, intensely anguished at the loss of their former pleasures, such gods take rebirth in the hells.

As we make spiritual progress through our own efforts, we will naturally come to experience more and more pleasure as well as greater ease and confidence. Under such circumstances it is easy to forget that the fruits of the spiritual life are only ever the results of striving. Complacency easily sets in, and when it does we slowly begin to fall. The realm of the gods is a place of great danger for spiritual aspirants. For that reason, the Bodhisattva Avalokiteshvara appears in the world of the gods as a white Buddha, playing the melody of impermanence upon a lute. Only in this beautiful form can the message of universal impermanence come home to the intoxicated gods.

# 6

## THE ASURAS

WE COME NEXT to the realm of the asuras, the jealous gods or Titans. According to Indian legend, these are gods who were expelled from the Heaven of the Thirty-Three Gods (one of the heavens of the sphere of sense desire) by its king, Shakra, following a great battle for divine supremacy. They are powerful and grotesque warlike beings, who are constantly armoured and always ready for battle. Theirs is a fiercely competitive world, for the asuras do not only war with the gods; they constantly fight with one another as well. Here there is no love, no gentleness, and no trust. There are only temporary strategic alliances that are liable to break down at any moment. The asuras live in a harsh realm, bristling with armament.

The asuras are usually depicted at war with the gods – fighting for possession of the Wish-Granting Tree. This tree, the fruit of which grants all desires, has its roots in the asuras' realm, but it grows up into the realm of the gods, where it bears its magical fruit. Again and again the asuras fall upon the gods, grasping for happiness and delight, but the gods easily repel them and they fall back in disarray and either begin trying to chop down the tree, cutting off their own potential happiness at its root, or they begin to fight with one another, each vying for hierarchical supremacy.

Male asuras are ugly and muscle-bound; female asuras, who are often a cause of dissension among the males, are voluptuous and alluring. Both sexes are highly driven to sexual conquest.

The asuras are sometimes referred to as the jealous gods, as their longing to acquire the delights of the gods comes not so much from their own desire for pleasure as much as from a powerful sense of envy. They want those things because they cannot bear others to possess what they do not. The success of the gods leaves them feeling belittled. They need to feel themselves to be the centre of the universe, and whenever others possess what they do not they experience themselves as deprived.

The gods acquired the fruits of the wish-granting tree as the result of skilful past deeds. The asuras have no time for that; they want the whole world and they want it now! By whatever means.

Seen from the psychological perspective, the asura realm describes the highly competitive psychological type. Asuras put an enormous amount of energy into maintaining their position at the top of any hierarchy. They always have to be the best

– the strongest, the richest, the fastest, the cleverest. One can find such people in profusion in the worlds of politics and business and also in the military, and among criminals, as well as in the 'glamour' industries, such as film and the media.

Asuras naturally form themselves into rigid hierarchical structures, but they strive always to rise in the hierarchy and tend only to relate to others in terms of dominance or submission, rarely in terms of equality.

While the male asura generally uses brute force and cunning to achieve his ends, the female asura usually uses her 'feminine wiles'. She manipulates her prey through the emotions, often using sexual fascination to bait her traps. The male asura usually wants to order the world about himself, turning it into a masculine hierarchy centring upon himself as the Cosmic King. The female asura, if she cannot dominate through her sexuality, might try to form her world into a vast family, centring upon herself as the Great Mother, with everyone, male and female, in a state of infantile dependence upon her.

Avalokiteshvara appears in the world of the asuras as a green Buddha, holding aloft the sword of wisdom. Asuras understand swords, at least to some extent. Using one as an example, the Buddha tells them that it is only through true understanding, through spiritual insight, that they will ever be able to make the conquests that will yield their heart's desire.

*Though one might conquer in battle thousands upon thousands, He who conquers himself is truly the greatest in battle.*[5]

Like all swords, the sword of wisdom is destructive, only in this case it destroys ignorance, cuts through delusion, and sets us free from vain attachment.

# 7

## THE PRETAS

NEXT WE COME to the world of the pretas. These desperate beings occupy a realm of startling aridity, a bleak desert of rock and sand through which flows a slow brackish river. There are only a few leafless trees to give shelter from the chill wind that blows through this realm. The occupants of this world are piteous, ungainly creatures, the colour of smoke. Their distended bodies are frail and insubstantial. Spindly arms and legs protrude from a swollen torso that culminates in a bloated, sagging belly. Their heads are carried upon long, constricted necks, and have eyes as large as saucers and tiny pin-prick mouths. Filled with pain and longing, they stare into the world with a blank gaze of endless yearning.

The pretas' overwhelming experience is one of unsatisfied desire. Whatever they manage to get into their tiny mouths instantly turns to excrement, ashes, or flames. As soon as their dry mouths approach the water that flows through their realm, it recedes from them. The tiny fruits on the meagre trees are almost always out of reach, but when they do manage to pluck one to eat it turns to swords and daggers in their bellies. This is the world of neurotic desire.

Neurotic desires are misplaced cravings, and they manifest in many different ways in contemporary Western life. We want affection so we eat chocolate. We want security, so we buy new trainers. The tendency to function in this sort of way may be quite

deep-seated – our mother always gave us chocolate when she approved of us; or it may be more superficial – the ads tell us that Nike guarantees security, but whatever its basis the fundamental mechanism is the same: seeking one thing we try to consume another. We look in the wrong place. New trainers never bring security, chocolate cannot replace affection, and so neurotic desires remain constantly unfulfilled.

The habit of neurotic, addicted desire is validated in some ways in our culture and condemned in others. Western culture elevates the value of neurotic, romantic attachment ('love'). Advertisements spur us on to ever greater feats of consumerism. Careers are built upon our attachment to status. At the same time, we look down on alcoholism and drug-addiction. Yet the fundamental mechanisms of all these are the same. We all seek stability, security, lasting pleasure, and painlessness in ways that are completely incapable of providing them.

Avalokiteshvara, appearing as a red Buddha in the preta realm, offers the beings there real food and drink. In other words, when we are in a state of deep addiction we need to be given what it is that we are really looking for.

Our constant sense of lack is an inevitable consequence of our basic incompleteness. We are not complete because 'we' do not really exist as such. There is no fixed, stable, unchanging ego-identity that we can point to and claim as our own. We are always changing, and therefore never more than provisional. Looking for stability in the round of change, we are constantly thwarted. The only true security available to us is the security that comes from realizing that we do not need to cling, that change is inevitable, and that change is, in the end, all right. Only by letting go of our attachments can we ever be free of the pain of neurotic clinging.

# 8

## THE HELLS

LIKE DANTE'S INFERNO, the Buddhist hell is divided into many sub-planes, each of which exists as the karmic outcome of particular unskilful acts. The hells are engulfed in flames and in each section presiding demons inflict a variety of torments on their unfortunate victims. Murderers and torturers are spitted upon sharp spikes and their guts are pecked by birds with steel beaks; the corrupters of the innocent are mired in slime and slowly devoured by huge maggots.

Buddhist teachers in the past have never hesitated to use images such as these to spur their followers to practice –

*Screaming in agony as his entire skin is ripped away by Yama's minions, his body infused in copper molten in the heat of the oblation-bearing fire, segments of his flesh cleaved away by the hundredfold blows of blazing swords and pikes, he drops repeatedly onto the red-hot ground of iron in consequence of his wrong deeds.*

*So, desire for what is good must be created, meditating carefully upon these things.*[6]

So writes Shantideva, in his *Bodhicharyavatara*, a beautifully poetic manual of instruction for living the altruistic Buddhist life.

The Buddhist hells, unlike their Christian counterparts, are not eternal. And Buddhist societies have somehow avoided falling into the mental states of gloom-ridden self-

righteousness that often prevail where the theistic hells are stressed, perhaps because such teachings are always accompanied by practical teachings on the path of self-transcendence. But however one takes this, one thing is clear – hellish states certainly do exist, if not below then above ground.

There are the hells-on-earth that we find in war zones and places of acute poverty, and there are hells-within, where people suffer acute physical and mental anguish.

Appearing in the hells as a smoke-coloured Buddha, Avalokiteshvara sprinkles *amrita* on all the beings there. *Amrita* is a kind of divine nectar like ambrosia, a healing balm that brings solace to all. Sometimes, when one is in a hellish mental state or fiercely gripped by pain, what one needs above all is just some immediate respite.

But there is also a deeper meaning here. The *amritapada*, the deathless or eternal state, is another term for Nirvana. According to one of the Chinese traditions, each realm has a certain number of red (good) seeds, black (bad) seeds, and golden yellow (Buddha) seeds in it. Good seeds are our potential for pleasure, bad seeds our potential for pain, and Buddha seeds represent our potential for Enlightenment. The human realm contains an equal measure of all of these. The gods have more good seeds than bad, the hells and the pretas have more bad seeds than good but more Buddha seeds than the gods. (Asuras and animals have few Buddha seeds and not many good seeds either).

What this means is that when we experience great states of woe we are more likely to be really disillusioned with Samsara. This 'dis-illusionment', the loss or weakening of our illusions, is not the same as mere disgruntlement. The latter is self-centred and carping, the former involves at least a degree of insight into the true nature of things.

Dis-illusioned in that way, we can begin to make a significant effort to change ourselves for the better. However painful our mental states, however difficult our lives, we can be sure of two things. First, all mental states do eventually pass. Over time, change always happens. Second, we can be sure of the law of karma, so no skilful effort, however difficult to make and no matter how slight, is ever wasted. It is this law that ensures that, if we consistently make an effort to change our mental states, then our progress off the wheel is guaranteed, sooner or later.

# 9

## THE ANIMALS

THE ANIMAL REALM contains all the many animals we know of – cats, dogs, cows, donkeys, lions, and mice. The main characteristic of the animal realm is its lack of the quality of highly developed self-awareness that differentiates humans from all other animals.

Traditionally, the animal realm is said to be dominated by the threefold desire for food, sex, and sleep. When these desires are satisfied the animals are gentle and even tame, but if any one of them is frustrated they can become wild and ferocious.

For human beings, the animal realm represents an overriding concern with the affairs of the body to the exclusion of higher matters. Such concerns have their place; there is nothing intrinsically wrong with having a body and, if we are to be healthy, its needs must be met. But for the animal-like human being the fulfilment of such needs becomes the sole aim of life. People in this state are not necessarily stupid. They may lead relatively sophisticated lives, operating complex technology, for example, or running successful businesses, but so long as their goals in life do not reach beyond the satisfaction of their own need for comfort they have not advanced beyond this stage of being.

The blue Buddha in the animal realm shows the animals a book. One of the key differences between ourselves and the other animals on this planet is our possession

of a developed culture. Cultural life stands as an intermediary between savagery and spiritual life. It is very difficult to pass from a state of ignorant barbarism straight into a commitment to spiritual practice without being first refined by an exposure to human culture.

In the past, Buddhism was always a bearer of culture as well as religion, and, with one major exception, wherever it spread in the East it took its previous cultural inheritance along with it. In that way the secular, humanistic culture it took with it was able to provide a foundation for the higher spiritual life. Only in China did Buddhism encounter a culture as highly developed as ours is today.

The task that Western Buddhists now face is twofold. First, we need to preserve the best of Western culture from the stultifying forces that are at work within it. In our great, levelling, consumerist age the treasures of our Western culture inheritance are under constant threat. There is the commercial pressure of commodification on the one hand, and that of disrespect and disregard on the other.

Secondly, we need to find out what in our cultural heritage helps and what hinders Dharma practice. With Western culture we have a great resource at our disposal. The great music, literature, and visual arts that we have inherited have a tremendous capacity for producing refined mental states. But, rooted in their respective theistic backgrounds, they come to us freighted with often unhelpful notions, such as 'original sin'.

Westerners who wish to embark on the spiritual path these days often also need to embark on a process of cultural education. Once we are able to see beyond the ideological, often theological, background that gave rise to them, we can use the great artefacts of Western cultural life to help us to develop stronger and more refined positive mental states. To the extent that we can do this, we can lift ourselves out of the animal realm which is, to some degree at least, something of an apparently comfortable resting place for many of us.

# 10

## THE HUMANS

HERE WE SEE human beings going about their human business. They buy, sell, meet, and talk. They engage in farming, commerce, the arts, leisure, and spiritual practice. They are born and they die.

The human realm is characterized by its peculiar centrality. The constant pain and frustrated desire for satisfaction experienced by the asuras, pretas, hell-beings, and animals numbs their minds and curbs their initiative. The gods are intoxicated with pleasure to the point of complete complacency. Humans, on the other hand, experience joy and pain in almost equal measure. Truly human consciousness is neither ecstatic like that of the gods nor agonized, like that of the beings in hell. It is neither fiercely competitive like the asuras, neurotically desirous like the pretas, nor mindlessly sensual like the animals. The beings in all these states can do little more than wait until the karma that produced the states they experience subsides. Humans have the capacity to act for the good.

In the human state we are aware of ourselves and others. We are able to satisfy, in a reasonable manner, our objective human needs, but we see that these have their limitations, and that there can be more to life. In this state, therefore, we are able to devote ourselves to spiritual development. This truly human state is one which most 'human beings' only intermittently, or perhaps never, experience.

In the human world a saffron-coloured Buddha carries a begging-bowl and a staff with three rings. These are the insignia of the religious mendicant, and what this means is that once we have achieved the human state our next task is to take up the spiritual life.

According to Buddhist thought, the human state is not easily achieved. In the *Chiggala Sutta*,[7] the Buddha made this point to a gathering of his followers. He asked them to suppose that the whole earth was covered in water. They were then to suppose that a man tossed a yoke with a single hole in it into the water. The yoke was driven here and there across the waters by all the great winds that pushed it. They then had to imagine that a blind turtle lived in that ocean. Once every hundred years it came up to the surface. Would that turtle, he asked them, stick his neck into the yoke with one hole?

'That would be a sheer coincidence,' they replied.

'In the same way,' the Buddha said, 'it is a sheer coincidence that one obtains the human state.'

However we wish to take this story, one thing is clear. Being human, we have the chance to make a great deal of our lives. Alternatively, we can languish and simply let the currents of our karma sweep us where they will. The human state represents a truly precious opportunity. What we make of it will depend to some extent at least on how much we understand the mechanisms that drive Samsara. These are outlined, as they apply to processes of rebirth, in the next section, which depicts the twelve links of conditioned co-production.

# 11

# THE TWELVE LINKS

THE TWELVE NIDANAS, or 'links', in the chain of conditioned co-production make up the rim of the Wheel. A blind man walking with the help of a stick; a potter throwing pots on his wheel; a monkey climbing a flowering tree; four people sitting in a boat; a house with five windows and a door; a couple embracing; a man with an arrow in his eye; a woman offering a man a drink; a man gathering fruit from a tree; a pregnant woman; a woman giving birth; and a corpse.

These twelve images between them set out an allegorical representation – perhaps originally devised for teaching purposes – of the way in which a new moment of consciousness first arises as a result of past conditions. That consciousness, with all its various faculties, apprehends the world in a certain way, and that gives rise to feelings of craving or aversion. These cause us to grasp on to the world (or push it away), and as a result of this process we become attached to a certain way of being. And so we are born and we die. Over and over. The Wheel just rolls on and on.

This teaching is traditionally used to explain how we move from lifetime to lifetime. It is also used to show how our mental states, and the worlds we consequently inhabit, change from moment to moment. The great fourth-century commentator Buddhaghosa eloquently described how, from the Enlightened perspective, change is all there is – birth and death take place again and again in every passing instant.

*In the ultimate sense the life-moment of living beings is extremely short, being only as much as the occurrence of a single conscious moment. Just as a chariot wheel, when it is rolling, rolls only on one point of its tyre, and, when it is at rest, rests only on one point, so too, the life of living beings lasts only for a single conscious moment. When that consciousness has ceased, the being is said to have ceased....*

*'Life, person, pleasure, pain – just these alone*
*Join in one conscious moment that flicks by.*
*Ceased aggregates of those dead or alive*
*Are all alike, gone never to return.*
*No (world is) born if (consciousness is) not*
*Produced; when that is present, then it lives;*
*When consciousness dissolves, the world is dead:*
*The highest sense this concept will allow.'*
*This is how death should be recollected as to the shortness of the moment.*[8]

Let us go back to our friend John. We left him shattered by the news of Jenny's betrayal. He never considered how ready *he* was to betray Bill. That is because John, like most of us, suffers from a deep spiritual ignorance that keeps him believing, usually unconsciously, that he is the single centre of this whole turning world. That is the first link – ignorance.

As a result of this ignorance, John's behaviour is largely blind and habitual. That is the second link – our unenlightened habitual propensities.

When John comes back from work and listens to Beethoven, he becomes one kind of man, with one kind of consciousness; when he slumps in front of the television he becomes another. This is the third link – consciousness.

Depending on what habits he gives way to, his whole mind-body complex and his whole world change. These are the fourth, fifth, and sixth links – the mind-body complex, the senses, and contact with the world.

Depending on what he has contact with, John has different feelings (the seventh link), and as a result he has different cravings (the eighth link). Usually, he just gives way to these. If he thinks about food he immediately feels like a snack, so he wanders off to the fridge. When he feels bored he craves stimulation and just picks up the paper. This is the ninth link – grasping.

John tends not to think of the consequences of his actions. But each act sets another process in train. When he clicks on the remote control with his left hand while mindlessly putting the tenth tortilla chip into his mouth with the right, John enters the animal world. When he closely attends to Beethoven, he enters the god world. This is the tenth link – becoming.

But each world just comes into being and passes away again, with very little conscious intervention from John. Like most of us he just drifts, from state to state, realm to realm, blown by the winds of his karma. Over and over and over again, we cycle in a round of changing states, all of them by and large unsatisfying. These are the eleventh and twelfth links – birth and death.

Fortunately, this is not the only way things can be. With attention we can change things for the better – even radically so. How that works we will see in the next section. Before that we need to examine each of the twelve links in more detail.

But first, a word of warning. We need to be careful how we approach this teaching. Above all, we are not to take it too literally. We are dealing with an allegory here, not a fixed and rigid mechanism. The Buddha used the idea of a chain of conditionally linked events to show how what passes through our minds determines what we become. Although he most often seems to have used the twelve-link formula to do this, he sometimes taught using five- or ten-link chains as well. Like all the lists in Buddhism, the twelve-link chain is instrumental. Its purpose is to illuminate the principle of conditionality and to illuminate some of the processes at work within it. No formula in itself definitively describes reality.

The material we will be looking at here can seem at first sight to be highly 'technical', but in fact it is more down to earth than that. It is part of the Buddhist attempt to describe how our own individual experiences work, how such experiences come to us, and how, through our own behaviour, we determine the quality of our lives. At each stage in the process we can refer to our own experience to see the meaning of what is being talked about.

## 1. IGNORANCE

The blind man walking with the help of a stick stands for *avidya*, or 'ignorance'. Theoretically, we could start our journey around the Wheel from any juncture, but tradition usually begins it here, at the fundamental root of our unenlightened state, for the ignorance referred to here is spiritual ignorance. This is not ignorance in the normal sense of the term. One may know a very great deal about the world and still be shrouded in spiritual ignorance.

Spiritual ignorance takes many forms. It amounts to a lack of insight into the true nature of reality, a blindness to how things really are, and its roots are as much emotional and volitional as intellectual. For example, the deeply-held conviction, that many of us share, that we can be made happy by just getting enough of Samsara is a profound instance of ignorance. Even if we were to win £10 million in the National Lottery, our acute sense of incompleteness would not be assuaged. Or else we tend to believe that situations can somehow be made permanent – our friends and lovers will always love us, our home will always be there to return to. Or we believe that we have, somewhere in our depths, a real self, our own true nature, that is somehow us-in-our-essence, which others must accept and which we can rely on. Or we believe in the existence of a creator god who can provide us with what we need and who must at all costs be appeased. All these beliefs are, according to Buddhism, examples of spiritual ignorance.

## 2. KARMA FORMATIONS

In dependence upon such spiritual ignorance, the *samskaras*, 'karma formations', arise. This is illustrated by the potter throwing pots on a wheel. These 'karma formations' are our deeply-rooted habits. According to the Buddha, *avidya*, the state of spiritual ignorance, is akin to drunkenness. The *samskaras* are like the actions we perform in that state. They are our unenlightened propensities. Under their sway we do, say, and think all kinds of things that we may even consider to be wise – but we have all seen drunks who think they are wise.

The *samskaras* are the energetic forces that create the well-worn tracks down which our lives proceed; they form the paths of least resistance that we tend unconsciously to follow. Looking back over time, we can recognize the habitual unfolding patterns that mark out the general drift and tendency of our lives. These are the signs that point to our deep underlying *samskaras* – the whole mass of our unconscious habits.

Having been ignorant, and having acted on that basis, karma has accrued. The first two links are thought of as the 'cause process' of the previous life or moment. What we now are is the result of what we did in the past. The next five links describe what we now become. They unfold the 'result process' of the present life, or moment.

### 3. CONSCIOUSNESS

In dependence upon the *samskaras* arises *vijnana* – 'consciousness'. This is symbolized by a monkey climbing a flowering tree. The term 'consciousness' is being used here in a peculiar sense. It represents the 're-linking' consciousness when the first moment of consciousness in the present existence is sparked into life, conditioned by the last moment of consciousness of the previous life. The monkey swings from branch to branch – consciousness passes from existence to existence. But we must beware, here, of taking this image too literally. The consciousness which moves from existence to existence is not unchanged in the process. What comes next is neither exactly the same as, nor entirely different from, what went before, but arises in dependence upon it.

### 4. NAME AND FORM

This re-linking consciousness is, as it were, holographic. Like a seed, it has, enfolded within it, significant elements of what we now become, for in dependence upon *vijnana* arises 'name and form' – *nama-rupa*, the mind-body complex.

This link is traditionally shown as a boat with four passengers, one of whom is steering. The boat is *rupa* – 'form' or 'corporeality'. The four passengers are *vedana* – 'feeling'; *samjna* – 'perception'; *samskaras* – 'volitions'; and *vijnana* – 'consciousness'. Consciousness is steering.

These five factors are the five *skandhas*, the five 'heaps' or 'aggregates' into which the Buddha resolved the whole human psychophysical organism. These five *skandhas* are not five 'things', which can each exist separately from one another, such as the body of a car and its four wheels. Rather, they are a collection of interdependent shifting processes that go to make up a human being constantly in flux. They are what we, with all our changing experiences, in the end come down to.

*Rupa*, 'form', describes what we perceive with our senses. It is what catalyses our senses into operation. I see a single yellow rose in the vase on my desk. The rose is the objective, or *rupa*, component of the experience.

*Vedana*, 'feeling', applies to the pleasant, painful, or neutral feelings that accompany sensations and emotions. I like roses, they usually provoke pleasant *vedana* in me.

*Samjna*, 'perception', consists in the process of recognizing and assimilating the sensations that are presented to us. I recognize the rose as a rose. I separate it from the mass of surrounding experiences.

*Samskara* (used here in a different sense from that in which we encountered it as the second link) means 'volition', or 'motivation'. After evaluating our sensations, volitions arise. I keep on gazing at the rose – it is a pleasant experience that I want to repeat.

*Vijnana*, 'consciousness', the last of the five *skandhas*, is not the same as the 're-linking' consciousness we encountered as the third link. Here it means 'discriminating awareness' and, in the case of unenlightened human beings, creates the dualistic sense of there being distinct subjects and objects. I see the rose as ultimately separate from myself, separate from the world, and I imagine it as being somehow fixed and somewhat unchanging. I do not see that it exists, in all its beauty, as a changing pattern in the constantly moving flux of life and that, along with myself and all other beings, it plays its part in a vast web of living interdependence.

## 5. THE SIX SENSE ORGANS

In dependence on *nama-rupa* arise the six sense organs, or *shadayatanas*. These are symbolized by a house with five windows and a door. In Buddhist thought, the mind is itself a sense organ, so the six senses are those of sight, sound, smell, taste, touch, and the mind. As a result of all that has gone before we have a certain capacity to experience the world. We have human senses, dogs have dog senses, and mosquitoes have mosquito senses. Our senses condition the way we apprehend the world. Indeed, they condition the world we apprehend. Were we mosquitoes, we would apprehend the mosquito world – a very different sort of place to this human world.

### 6. CONTACT

In dependence on the six sense organs arises 'contact' or *sparsha*. This is shown by a man and woman embracing. Because we have the six human senses the human world impinges upon us.

### 7. FEELING

In dependence upon contact, *vedana* or feeling arises. This is shown by a man with an arrow stuck in his eye. As a result of our contact with the world, arise feelings – whether pleasant, painful, or neutral. Every sensation is accompanied by a feeling tone and the vast mass of sensations that make up our contact with the world therefore carry with them a large complex of feelings that make up the overall feeling tone of that moment of experience.

This is a crucial juncture, so it is worth summing up a little here. To begin with, we had ignorance giving rise to the karma formations. These two links made up the cause process of the past. As a consequence of these, there arose a result process in the present.

This began with a first moment of consciousness that unfolded into the five *skandhas*. The six senses came into being, and these determined the nature of our interaction with the world. This interaction may please us or it may not, but there is nothing we can do about it. We cannot go back and change the past, and what happens in this present moment is the immutable result of the past. We cannot change the past, but we can do something about the future. The past is closed and there really is no point whatsoever in crying over the milk we have spilled. Instead, we should turn our attention to what is to come, for the future is completely open.

What happens next on the Wheel is therefore of immense spiritual significance, for, having exhausted the result process of the present, we are about to embark on the cause process of the future. We are about to begin the process of bringing a new self and a new world into being. If, as we usually do, we give way at this point to craving (or aversion), we will stay bound to the Wheel. If, on the other hand, we reflect on the reality of our situation, and note that our cravings are endless and never provide us with any real satisfaction, we begin to escape from the Wheel. How that process works we will see later on. In the meantime, we will stay with the Wheel and complete the next five links, for here we can see, in slow motion as it were, what normally seems just to happen, unconsciously. For what happens next, usually without reflecting even a little upon it, is that we propel ourselves into a new life.

## 8. CRAVING

In dependence upon feeling, craving or *trishna* arises. This is represented by a woman offering a drink to a seated man. *Trishna*, which also means 'thirst', is traditionally seen as manifesting in three different ways. There is craving for sense experience, craving for continued existence, and craving for non-existence or death. It is the response of the personality to the pleasant, painful, or neutral feelings that preceded the craving. We want pleasant feelings to continue, painful feelings to go away, and neutral feelings to be pleasant. We respond with desire or dislike to whatever event precipitated the feeling in the first place.

As we saw earlier, our cravings are rooted in the very depths of our being. In a certain sense, they define us. 'I want this, I don't want that.' This delineates the outlines of our personality, it makes us what we think we are and helps to give us a fixed sense of ourselves and a feeling of security in the midst of the sea of change.

## 9. GRASPING

In dependence upon craving, grasping or attachment, *upadana*, arises. This is represented by a man gathering fruit from a tree. We want more. We move towards the objects of our desires – chocolate bars and beautiful people; away from what we dislike – ugliness and discomfort. Unconsciously believing that the objects of our cravings are capable of providing us with true and lasting satisfaction, we reach out and try to attach ourselves to them, or eliminate them from our worlds, all the time. But *upadana* also has more subtle dimensions. We can be attached to people, to things, and to different kinds of pleasing sense experience, but we can also be attached to 'views': opinions, beliefs, and speculations. We can be attached to a narrow sense of ethics and to ritual observances seen as ends in themselves. And of course we can be attached to a sense of ourselves as a fixed unchanging ego-identity. But however subtly these attachments manifest, they each of them serve to keep us bound to the Wheel of Life. In a continuous movement of attraction and repulsion, now clinging to this, now to that, over and over, we dance the dance of rebirth.

### 10. BECOMING

In dependence on grasping, becoming or *bhava* arises. This is symbolized by a pregnant woman. This link is interpreted differently by different Buddhist traditions. You can see it as representing the completion of the causal process of the present, or you could see it as representing the first link in the result process of the future. In any event, what it represents at its most general is the arising of a fresh existential situation. A new situation emerges. When I give way to my fantasies about winning the lottery I become mildly obsessed with unfulfilled desires and enter the world of the hungry ghosts; when I give way to my anger I become more like an asura and I enter that world for a time. All my apparently subjective mental states have their subtle counterpart in the apparently objective world in which I live and move. When I am smiling and happy, people smile back at me and the world I live in is a happier place. The subjective and the objective, self and the world, arise together.

### 11. AND 12. BIRTH AND DEATH

Finally, we come to the last two links in the chain – the result process of the future: a woman giving birth – representing *jati*, or 'birth'; and a corpse – representing *jara-marana*, decay and death. That is what the future holds for us. We will be born and we will die. New situations will come into being and then they will pass away, over and over, as long as we are attached to the Wheel. Some situations will be pleasant, some will be painful, but all will be essentially marked with the same fundamental characteristic: none of them will give us lasting satisfaction.

Due to our ignorance and the actions that followed from it, a new seed of consciousness arises. That seed unfolds in the form of a particular psychophysical organism, endowed with the six senses, which make contact with the six sense objects. As a result, feelings arise and we start to crave. We try to cling on to those feelings that are pleasant, while rejecting those that are unpleasant, and so, attached to the world of conditioned existence, we precipitate ourselves into another and yet another similar situation in the future – thus remaining subject to suffering, old age, disease, death.

# 12

# THE SPIRAL PATH

FORTUNATELY FOR US, we live at a time when a Buddha has appeared in the world. Buddhas show us how we can escape the grip of the ever-turning Wheel. Shakyamuni, the Buddha of our era, had a great deal to say about this subject. Among many other things, he taught that there is what my teacher Sangharakshita has termed a Spiral Path, which leads onwards and upwards away from the Wheel. One of the most popular accounts of this path is that found in the *Samyutta-Nikaya*.[9] Whereas on the 'cyclic' twelve-link chain we have just looked at, beings circle round and around at more or less the same level of existence – where pain gives way in time to pleasure, pleasure to pain, in a process of reaction between opposites – on the spiral path each successive link augments the one that precedes it.

On the Spiral Path one moves from suffering to faith to joy, then rapture, serenity, bliss, concentration, knowledge and vision of things as they really are, disentanglement, dispassion, and liberation. How this works in detail, we shall examine in this section.

We put a great deal of effort into bemoaning facts of life over which we have no control. 'If only the sun was shining ... I won the lottery ... my wife had loved me more ... I lived in Ipanema ... I was five inches taller ... I was able to dance and sing ... I had been kinder to my daughter ... then everything would be all right.' This is a profound waste of time and it represents a deflection of our attention from the things over which we *do* have some control.

As the twelve cyclic links demonstrate, actions from the past bring about results in the present. The situation we currently face, at this precise instant in the present, is an outcome of all that has gone before. It is what it is and it cannot be other than that. There is absolutely nothing that we can do to change this precise moment in time. What we *can* do is act so that the next instant is better. The present moment is immutable – the future is completely open.

As a result of all that has gone before us, we find ourselves facing a particular situation in the present and we have certain feelings about it. Say we are walking down the road to the shops. The sun is shining and we are happy to be there. Or perhaps it is raining and we are a bit miserable. Or perhaps we do not really feel anything very much. In any case, even in such simple situations as these, feelings always arise and these are either pleasant, painful, or neutral.

Most of the time we react to pleasant feelings with craving. If we have a pleasant experience, our natural tendency is to try to repeat it. We are rarely content just to let pleasant feelings come and go. If the feelings are unpleasant, painful, or simply unsatisfactory then, instinctively, we try to push them away. This is aversion. If we are confronted by a feeling that is neither pleasant nor painful, then we are bewildered. We do not know whether to grasp it or reject it.

We react in one of these three ways all the time, to all the sensations, feelings, and experiences that continually arise through all the senses and the mind. In this way, a new result process succeeds the previous, reactive, cause process and the Wheel of Life makes one more revolution. All the conditions are created for a fresh rebirth. This very point, in the present, where in dependence upon feelings arises craving, is where it all happens.

What if we do not react in this way? What if, when feelings arise, we do not react with craving, or aversion, or bewilderment? It is then that we enter the path to Nirvana, for Nirvana is marked by the cessation of craving. This, however, is not very easy to do.

There are two ways to ensure that feeling is not succeeded by craving. There is a 'sudden way', when the Wheel is, as it were, shattered with a single blow, and a 'gradual way', in which, little by little, it is slowed down.

The sudden way is illustrated by a story from the *Udana*.[10] A monk called Bahiya came to where the Buddha was staying. He badly wanted to meet the Buddha. In fact, he had travelled many hundreds of miles, without rest, to see him, so desperate was he to receive his teachings. When Bahiya arrived, however, the Buddha was out on his daily almsround. Bahiya could not wait for his return and, without even resting for a moment, he discovered where the Buddha had gone and followed him. Before long Bahiya caught up with the Buddha. Walking just behind him, as he went begging from door to door, Bahiya called out, 'Please give me a teaching.' But it was the Buddha's custom that he never spoke while on his almsround, so he said nothing and walked quietly on. Bahiya asked a second time, even more urgently, 'Please give me a teaching.' But the Buddha ignored him and walked on. Then Bahiya asked a third time.

Now it was another of the Buddha's customs that if anyone asked him something a third time, whatever the question and however terrible the consequences might be for the questioner, he would answer it. So he stopped in his tracks, turned around, gave Bahiya a direct look and said, 'In the seen, only the seen. In the heard, only the heard. In the touched, only the touched. In the tasted, only the tasted. In the smelt, only the smelt. In the thought, only the thought.' He then turned around and continued on his almsround. And Bahiya became Enlightened on the spot.

This is the sudden way. The Buddha said, in effect, 'Do not react.' 'In the heard, only the heard.' If a sound impinges on your eardrums, that is just a sound. You do not have to react to that sound – you do not have to like it or not like it; you do not have to want it to continue or to stop. Similarly with all the senses; you need not react; you can simply allow the bare experience to be there, fully attending to it, fully in the present. If you can do that, you transcend Samsara in a flash. You are no longer attached to the Wheel.

But this is not at all easy to do, so it is fortunate for us that there is also a gradual way. This gradual way is the path of continuous spiritual progress. It is marked by increasing mindfulness and awareness, by increased ethical sensitivity, and by increased emotional positivity. It has been characterized, in the Buddha's teachings, by many different formulas: there is the Threefold Way of ethics, meditation, and wisdom; the Noble Eightfold Path; the Seven Stages of Purification; the Six Perfections; and so on. But in the context of the twelve links of the Wheel of Life, the formula that is of greatest interest to us is one that relates directly to it. This is the formula of the Spiral Path. This also has twelve links, but in this case the links are not cyclic. Instead, they are augmentative.

While on the Wheel, we are caught up in an endless process of reaction between opposites. Happiness gives way to sadness, pleasure to pain, pain to pleasure. So we revolve, on and on. On the Spiral Path, however, each succeeding link represents an intensification of the positivity of the preceding one – joy gives way to rapture, rapture to calm, calm to bliss, and so on in an ever-increasing spiral of spiritual positivity that culminates, ultimately, in Nirvana. For this reason we can speak of the Spiral Path as the path of twelve positive links.

In order to see how this works in practice, let us have another look at our friend John. We left him in a state of quite acute suffering (Jenny had just left him for his old colleague and rival Bill). Since then, John has found his life to be more and more unsatisfying. It is not just that he has no girl-friend – he knows he could get another in time – or that confronting Bill's smug sympathy in the office every day is tiresome – he could get another job. There is more to it than that. It is just that ever since Jenny left him he has been wondering what his life is all about.

Yes, he has a few pleasures – he likes fine wines, tennis, music; and yes, he is good at his job, and paid much more than his father ever was; but where is it all going? What is life all about? Surely there must be more to it than that....

These are the first two links in the spiral path: suffering, or just plain unsatisfactoriness, and the first flickering of faith – the sense that there must be more than just this.

Idly leafing through a *What's On* magazine at home one evening, John notices a small ad in the listing section: 'Free Buddhist meditation classes.' Hmm ... there might be something in that. John remembers once, when he was still at school, he sat down in the break and, somehow, fell into a deep reverie. He seemed to become much calmer, quieter, and happier; somehow more focused. He has always wondered if that had some link with meditation. And Buddhism itself is kind of interesting. The Dalai Lama always comes across as a thoroughly decent man ... not stuffy or puffed up. Perhaps it is worth giving this Buddhist meditation a go.

So John goes to his first meditation class. He likes the people he meets, enjoys the meditation, finds it really making a difference to his life, and he gets more deeply involved in it all. As he learns more about Buddhism, John begins to take up the five precepts of Buddhist ethics. He undertakes to refrain from harming things, but instead to cultivate kindness; to refrain from taking what is not given and instead to cultivate generosity; to refrain from hurting others through his sexual behaviour and instead to cultivate contentment; not to lie, but to cultivate truthfulness; and finally, avoiding intoxication, to cultivate clarity.

As time passes, John increasingly feels the benefits of his practice of ethics and meditation. He feels so much clearer and he has a light, easy conscience. He just seems to grow happier and happier. In fact, these days he sometimes finds that joy just wells up inside him, almost for no reason. He is happy when it's sunny, he is happy when it rains. It is good to be here on this planet. It is good just to be alive.

This is the third link on the Spiral Path. The experience of joy and innocent delight.

Now John is convinced that Buddhism and meditation is for him. In time he commits himself to going off into the countryside on a long meditation retreat. Here, in the context of a silent retreat, he finds his meditation going deeper and deeper. At times, thrills of rapture rise up his spine, undoing all the old knots of tension. This is the fourth link. Then, still meditating, still concentrated, the rapture seems to expand and radiate outwards. It spills over into a vast still lake of meditative silence, where it is absorbed, pacified, and transcended.

John passes for a time into a state of profound serenity. This is the fifth link. Out of this serenity feelings of intense bliss well up from the depths of his being. This is the sixth link. Now he is fully present, fully integrated, fully concentrated. His whole psychophysical organism is completely one-pointed. This is the seventh link.

With a mind that is now concentrated, purified, bright, pliant, malleable, and imperturbable, John begins to allow thoughts and feelings to arise within him. 'All conditioned things are impermanent,' he reflects, 'they are insubstantial and ultimately unsatisfactory.' Deeper and deeper he penetrates into the reality of what he is saying. It is true, so true. How could he ever have thought otherwise? John begins to laugh, great rolls of laughter that start at the very bottom of his being and roll on out over the retreat centre – 'Of course, of course, how could he have thought otherwise? How could he *not* have thought otherwise?' He has begun to see things as they really are. This is the eighth link.

From now on John dedicates himself to simplifying his life and to making time for reflection. He works constantly at disentangling the complex connections that exist between the ego identity that he has now seen through and the world in which he lives and moves. This is the ninth link. He grows less and less concerned with mundane matters. This is the tenth link. And he knows with an absolute conviction that one day he will be totally free from the Wheel. He will achieve liberation, the eleventh link, and he will know that he has finally done so – the twelfth link.

That is the Spiral Path. As we saw, it begins with *duhkha*, 'pain', 'suffering', or 'unsatisfactoriness'. *Duhkha* corresponds, in the twelve links on the Wheel, to *vedana*, 'feeling' – the last link in the result process of the present.

Of course, the spiritual life is not as smooth for the vast majority of us as it was for John, nor do we usually move along it so quickly. Sometimes we go up, sometimes we go down. Sometimes we seem to spend many years even stuck in a kind of spiritual doldrums. But the Spiral Path nonetheless indicates very clearly the ultimately progressive nature of spiritual life. It may take a few years, it may take many lifetimes, but if we only keep up our efforts liberation is eventually assured.

In the course of our daily lives, sensations and feelings come at us from all sides. We usually react to them with craving and thus perpetuate the cyclic processes of the Wheel. But it need not be like that; we can, instead, respond positively. As all these sensations, feelings, and experiences – pleasant, painful, and neutral – impinge on us, we can begin to see that none of them, not even the pleasant ones, are really satisfactory.

Even if we could somehow isolate and perpetuate the pleasant experiences, and eliminate the painful ones, that would still not be enough, for we would still experience some sense of lack. Something in us would still not be satisfied. In some deep part of ourselves we would remain frustrated.

Once we begin to realize that the whole of conditioned existence – our life and our experience in the ordinary sense – is not enough, we are able to step on to the Spiral Path. When we see that life as we have been leading it cannot give us permanent, true satisfaction or happiness, that it is, in other words, *duhkha*, or unsatisfactory, then we are ready to embark on the path of spiritual transformation.

Once we see our everyday experience in this way we begin to sit loose to it, even to lose interest in it, and we start to think that there must be something higher, something beyond, that can give us deeper satisfaction. Eventually, we begin to shift our attention and gradually to place our heart (the Sanskrit word *shraddha*, 'faith', comes from a verb meaning 'to place the heart') not so much on the conditioned, on the things of everyday experience, but more and more upon the Unconditioned, on Nirvana. In this way faith develops.

At first, our faith may be a little vague, but it gradually strengthens and eventually becomes faith in the Buddha, the ideal of human Enlightenment; the Dharma, his teaching; and the Sangha, the spiritual fellowship of those who have made the teachings their own. These 'three jewels' come in time to be seen as the embodiments of our highest values, standing above and beyond the world but at the same time giving it meaning and significance. 'Placing the heart' more and more upon these, we begin increasingly to act in the light of the Buddha's teachings. Instead of craving arising in dependence upon feeling, faith arises in dependence upon unsatisfactoriness, and we enter the path to Nirvana. Faith stands on the Spiral as craving does on the Wheel. It is the first link in the cause process of the future.

Following on from faith arises *pramodya*, or 'satisfaction and delight'. This is the result of the awareness that you have nothing to reproach yourself with. It means having an easy conscience. When our behaviour accords with our ethical ideals, a sense of unity, harmony, and integration arises. There are two Buddhist practices that help a great deal in this respect.

First, there is the practice of following one or another of the Buddhist ethical codes. The most basic of these is the list of five precepts that John, and most Buddhists, adopt. But as long as we are unenlightened we will continue, from time to time, not to live up to our ethical ideals, and this fact can sometimes weigh us down. For this reason, the Buddha also encouraged the practice of confession where, with a friend or someone whom we respect spiritually, we simply make a clean breast of our own ethical failings, admit them, let go of them, and resolve to make more effort in the future. As a result of letting go of our failings in this way and of strengthening our sense of behaving in accordance with our ideals, our feelings of delight develop and grow stronger.

And then, in dependence on delight arises *priti* or 'rapture'. This point on the Spiral Path marks the transition from the world of sense desire. This transition is normally experienced in the context of meditation, or in any other still, absorbed activity. It arises naturally and spontaneously as concentration on an object becomes more and more intense and our attachment to sense experience is accordingly, temporarily at least, suspended.

*Priti* represents the deep sense of relief that comes about as the result of the liberation of the emotional energies that had been locked up in the deep-seated conflicts of the unconscious mind, and the experience of it can be very acute indeed. According to one commentary,

> *Rapture is of five kinds: the lesser thrill, momentary rapture, flooding rapture, all-pervading rapture and transporting rapture. Of these, the lesser thrill is only able to raise the hairs of the body; the momentary rapture is like the production of lightning moment by moment; like waves breaking on the seashore, the flooding rapture descends on the body and breaks;... when all-pervading rapture arises, the whole body is completely surcharged, blown like a full bladder or like a mountain cavern pouring forth a mighty flood of water;... the transporting rapture is strong, and lifts the body up to the extent of launching it in the air.*[11]

In order to move on in meditation from these intensely felt physical states, some degree of calm is needed. Thus, in dependence on rapture arises *prashrabdhi*, calm, repose, or tranquillity.

The traditional texts give an interesting illustration here. Suppose an elephant were to enter a small pond, not much larger than the elephant, water would then splash out of the pond on all sides. Likewise, if our rapture is great and our capacity to receive it is small, our energy will spill over in the form of physical responses mentioned above. But if the elephant were to step into a lake or a large river, he would do so with barely a ripple, for big as the elephant is, the body of water is even bigger. In the same way when one arrives at the state of calm, even though the rapture may have been very great one is able to receive it and the physical responses die down, leaving only the subtle, inner, emotional experience of calm where our attention is first disengaged and then simply withdrawn from the body and its concerns. This is not merely a passive state. Not only are the mind and body calmed, but by releasing all strains and tension, they are brought into a state of lightness, flexibility, adaptability, alertness, and directness. This is a state of extreme refinement and delicacy of feeling, in dependence upon which arises *sukha* or 'bliss'.

This is the feeling of intense happiness that wells up from the depths of our being when, in meditation, we are no longer aware of the physical body. It is an experience that is so enthralling and overwhelming that we can be occupied and absorbed in it for hours, even for days on end, to the exclusion of all other interests. But however natural, healthy, and intense the experience of meditative bliss may be, the Buddha advised us to be careful not to allow it to overpower our mindfulness in such a way that it becomes an end in itself.

We need to move on and, in dependence on bliss, *samadhi* or 'concentration' arises. This is an ethically positive one-pointedness (unlike the one-pointedness in the mind of the murderer about to act) and it corresponds to states of profound meditative absorption. This is the last of the mundane links on the Spiral Path, for after our concentration has been made complete, with a fully concentrated mind we come to see things as they really are and enter upon the transcendental path, from which spiritual regress is impossible.

In dependence on concentration arises *jnanadarshana*, 'knowledge and vision' (of things as they really are). It is important, above all, to bear in mind that this is essentially an experience – a powerful, direct, personal experience of the ultimate meaning of things. Such an experience is entirely transformative and is only very, very distantly akin to our ordinary day-to-day sense of intellectual understanding.

In dependence upon such insight arises *nirveda*, 'disgust' or 'withdrawal'. This is not simply a movement of recoil or withdrawal from the imperfections of the world in the ordinary psychological sense. Disgust and aversion are normally rooted in unhealthy mental states. *Nirveda* is more like a 'serene withdrawal' from our normal attachment to conditioned existence. It is like a traveller going about in the desert. He sees a mirage and, thinking he will soon be able to quench his thirst, he hurries towards it. But once he comes to see things as they really are, he sees through the mirage. He knows that it will not in any sense be able to give him what he wants, so he naturally withdraws his attention and loses interest in it. In the same way, once we see fully into the true nature of conditioned existence we see that it cannot give us what we really want, so we withdraw from our emotional attachment to all its many aspects.

In dependence upon withdrawal arises *vairagya*, 'dispassion'. This is a state of complete tranquillity. Here, we cannot be moved by any worldly event. It is a state of complete spiritual imperturbability. This is not a state of apathy, or stoical hardness, or insensitivity. Instead, it is one where our awareness of the true nature of reality is so complete that nothing is able to surprise or disturb us. We are simply rooted in awareness of things as they are, and we are therefore unshakeable.

In dependence on dispassion arises *vimukti*, 'liberation' or 'freedom'. This is freedom from all subjective, emotional, and psychological biases, as well as freedom from all wrong views, all ignorance, all philosophical speculation.

Here, the heart and mind are finally free from all attachments – even attachment to the distinction between Samsara and Nirvana – and one is thus free to move about as much in the one as in the other, acting always with compassion for the benefit of all.

Finally, in dependence on liberation arises *asravakshayajnana* or 'knowledge of the destruction of the biases' – that is, the biases towards sense desire, desire for continued existence, and spiritual ignorance.

Although this is traditionally phrased in a negative form, it is anything but a state of annihilation. The emphasis is on the *knowledge* of the destruction of the biases. Corresponding as this does to the absolutely ineffable state of Enlightenment itself, little can usefully be said here. We have arrived at the state of Buddhahood itself, the final goal of all spiritual striving.

This whole Spiral Path unfolds in a sense quite naturally, although not necessarily easily, once we begin to practise. As the Buddha put it in the *Anguttara-Nikaya* (working with a list of ten links this time),

> So you see, monks, revulsion and fading of interest have release by knowing and seeing as object and profit; seeing and knowing (things) as they really are, have revulsion and fading interest as object and profit; concentration has knowing and seeing things as they really are as object and profit; happiness has concentration as object and profit; calm has happiness; rapture has calm; joy has rapture; freedom from remorse has joy; good conduct has freedom from remorse as its object, freedom from remorse as its profit. Thus, monks, one state just causes another state to swell, one state just causes the fulfilment of another state, for the sake of going from the not-beyond to the beyond.[12]

'One state just causes another to swell, one state causes the fulfilment of another state....' All we have to do is begin. We start with 'good conduct', the practice of ethics. That leads, quite naturally and completely inevitably, to a sense of freedom from remorse. If we continue to practise ethics in that way, freedom from remorse naturally leads to joy, joy to rapture, and the whole Spiral Path opens out in front of us. And this all begins with the practice of ethics, at the point where feeling gives way to craving on the Wheel of Life. If only we can see that truth – that our cravings lead us not to satisfaction but simply to more of the same old stale unsatisfactoriness – then we can place our hearts upon the Three Jewels, the Buddha, the Dharma, and the Sangha, and embark on the greatest of all adventures: the path of the spiritual life.

# CONCLUSION

WE HAVE COME on quite a long journey in this book. We have seen how craving, aversion, and delusion – the cock, the snake, and the pig – drive the Wheel round and around. We have seen how our karma, our skilful or unskilful acts, determine what we next become; how we can dwell in the light of clarity or be blinded by the darkness of confusion. Our consciousness, we saw, is capable of divine mental states, but also hellish ones. We can be dull like animals, angry and envious like the anti-gods, neurotic like the pretas, or just plain human, with the capacity for choice.

We saw how the process of change works, how our consciousness changes from moment to moment or lifetime to lifetime in dependence on the way in which we respond to the feelings that arise within us. If we react to pleasant feelings with greed and painful ones with aversion we will just circle around and around the Wheel. But if we can just sit with the feelings that arise, acknowledging them for what they are, merely feelings, and if we can recollect that they are of themselves unable to give us any lasting satisfaction, we can then turn instead to the Spiral Path, which begins with suffering and ends with complete liberation.

It has been a long journey and we have had to absorb much information along the way. I hope that information proves to be useful. Above all, I hope that it encourages readers to try to put some of it into practice. What we all need to do is to seek out that tiny gap that arises in every moment of existence, the point where feeling gives way to craving. If we can only cultivate enough calm, clarity, and awareness to be aware of that gap when it opens and not to leap over it but, instead – reflecting on the pain and unsatisfactoriness that is inherent in the Wheel – just sit with it, then all manner of wonderful things may happen. Sitting in the present moment, turning away from our momentary feelings of craving, we do not have a great deal to lose. Rather, we have everything to gain.

# NOTES AND REFERENCES

1   e.g. the *Mula-Sarvastivada-Vinaya*. A version of the Wheel of Life is also described at *Vishuddhimagga* vii.7–8.
2   See Jataka 316.
3   Adapted from *Majjhima-Nikaya* 135.
4   Buddhaghosa, *The Atthasalini*, trans. Maung Tin in *The Expositor*, ed. C.A.W. Rhys Davids, Pali Text Society, London 1920, vol.ii, p.360.
5   Adapted from *Dhammapada* 103.
6   Shantideva, *The Bodhicharyavatara*, Kate Crosby and Andrew Skilton (trans.), Oxford University Press, Oxford 1996, p.71.
7   *Samyutta-Nikaya* v.455.
8   Buddhaghosa, *Visuddhimagga*, in Bhikkhu Nanamoli (trans.), *The Path of Purification* viii.39, Buddhist Publication Society, Kandy 1991, pp.233–4.
9   *Samyutta-Nikaya* ii.29–36.
10  F.L. Woodward (trans.), *The Minor Anthologies of the Pali Canon*, part ii: *Udana, Verses of Uplift and Itivuttaka, As It Was Said*, Pali Text Society, London 1985, pp.8–11. One of the older texts of the Pali Canon.
11  Buddhaghosa, *The Atthasalini*, trans. Maung Tin in *The Expositor*, ed. C.A.W. Rhys Davids, Pali Text Society, London 1920, vol.i, pp.153–4.
12  *Anguttara-Nikaya* v.3–4 in F.L. Woodward (trans.), *The Book of the Gradual Sayings*, vol.v, Pali Text Society, Oxford 1996. p.4.

# FURTHER READING

Sangharakshita, *The Three Jewels*, Windhorse, Birmingham 1998
Sangharakshita, *A Guide to the Buddhist Path*, Windhorse, Birmingham 1996
Rupert Gethin, *The Foundations of Buddhism*, Oxford University Press, Oxford 1998
Kulananda, *Western Buddhism*, Thorsons, London 1997
Alex Kennedy (Subhuti), *The Buddhist Vision*, Rider, London 1985

# INDEX

The Windhorse symbolizes the energy of the enlightened mind carrying the Three Jewels –
the Buddha, the Dharma, and the Sangha – to all sentient beings.

Buddhism is one of the fastest-growing spiritual traditions in the Western world.
Throughout its 2,500-year history, it has always succeeded in adapting its mode of expression
to suit whatever culture it has encountered.

Windhorse Publications aims to continue this tradition as Buddhism comes to the West.
Today's Westerners are heirs to the entire Buddhist tradition, free to draw instruction and
inspiration from all the many schools and branches. Windhorse publishes works by authors
who not only understand the Buddhist tradition but are also familiar with Western culture
and the Western mind. Manuscripts welcome.

For orders and catalogues please write to

| WINDHORSE PUBLICATIONS | WINDHORSE BOOKS | WEATHERHILL INC |
| --- | --- | --- |
| 11 PARK ROAD | P O BOX 574 | 41 MONROE TURNPIKE |
| BIRMINGHAM | NEWTOWN | TRUMBULL |
| B13 8AB | NSW 2042 | CT 06611 |
| UK | AUSTRALIA | USA |

Windhorse Publications is an arm of the Friends of the Western Buddhist Order, which has
more than sixty centres on five continents. Through these centres, members of the Western
Buddhist Order offer regular programmes of events for the general public and for more
experienced students. These include meditation classes, public talks, study on Buddhist
themes and texts, and 'bodywork' classes such as t'ai chi, yoga, and massage. The FWBO also
runs several retreat centres and the Karuna Trust, a fund-raising charity that supports social
welfare projects in the slums and villages of India.

Many FWBO centres have residential spiritual communities and ethical businesses associated
with them. Arts activities are encouraged too, as is the development of strong bonds of
friendship between people who share the same ideals. In this way the FWBO is developing a
unique approach to Buddhism, not simply as a set of techniques, less still as an exotic cultural
interest, but as a creatively directed way of life for people living in the modern world.

If you would like more information about the FWBO please visit www.fwbo.org or write to

| LONDON BUDDHIST CENTRE | ARYALOKA |
| --- | --- |
| 51 ROMAN ROAD | HEARTWOOD CIRCLE |
| LONDON | NEWMARKET |
| E2 0HU | NH 03857 |
| UK | USA |

# ALSO FROM WINDHORSE

**VESSANTARA**

**THE MANDALA OF THE FIVE BUDDHAS**

The mandala of the Five Buddhas is an important Buddhist symbol – a multi-faceted jewel communicating the different aspects of Enlightenment. Meeting each Buddha in turn, we start to awaken to the qualities they embody – energy, beauty, love, confidence, and freedom.

By contemplating the mandala as a whole we can transform ourselves through the power of the imagination, and experience the majesty of the mind set free.

Part of a series on *Buddhist symbols*.

*96 pages, with colour plates*
*ISBN 1 899579 16 8*
*£5.99/$11.95*

**BODHIPAKSA**

**VEGETARIANISM**

Part of a series on *Living a Buddhist Life*, this book explores connections between vegetarianism and the spiritual life.

As a trained vet, Bodhipaksa is well placed to reveal the suffering of animals in the farming industry, and as a practising Buddhist he can identify the ethical consequences of inflicting such suffering. Through the Buddhist teaching of interconnectedness he lays bare the effects our eating habits can have upon us, upon animals, and upon the environment.

He concludes that by becoming vegetarian we can affirm life in a very clear and immediate way, and so experience a greater sense of contentment, harmony, and happiness.

*112 pages*
*ISBN 1 899579 15 X*
*£4.99/$9.95*

JINANANDA

## MEDITATING

This is a guide to Buddhist meditation that is in sympathy with modern lifestyle. Accessible and thought-provoking, this books tells you what you need to know to get started with meditation, and keep going through the ups and downs of everyday life. Realistic, witty, and very inspiring.

*136 pages*
*ISBN 1 899579 07 9*
*£4.99/$9.95*

SANGHARAKSHITA

## TIBETAN BUDDHISM: AN INTRODUCTION

A glorious past, a traumatic present, an uncertain future. What are we to make of Tibetan Buddhism?

Sangharakshita has spent many years in contact with Tibetan lamas of all schools, within the context of a wide experience of the Buddhist tradition as a whole. He is admirably qualified as a guide through the labyrinth that is Tibetan Buddhism. In this book he gives a down-to-earth account of the origin and history of Buddhism in Tibet, and explains the essentials of this practical tradition which has much to teach us.

As the essence of Tibetan Buddhism is revealed, it is shown to be a beautiful and noble tradition which – and this is the important thing – can help us contact a sense of beauty and nobility in our lives.

*144 pages, illustrated*
*ISBN 0 904766 86 1*
*£8.50/$16.95*